There Once Was a Sky Full of Stars

for Joy, Jesse, and Makaela
— B.C.

for Jennifer, Mike, and Bill
— A.Z.

Words © 2010 Robert Crelin

Pictures © 2010 Amie Ziner

Published by Sky & Telescope Media, LLC
90 Sherman Street, Cambridge, MA 02140, USA
SkyandTelescope.com

Printed in China

Printed 2003, 2007, 2010

Library of Congress Cataloging-in-Publication Data

Crelin, Bob.
    There once was a sky full of stars / written by Bob Crelin ; illustrated by Amie Ziner.
        p. cm.
    Summary: A lyrical reminiscence for the time before electrical illumination made the
natural beauty of the night sky so hard to see.
    ISBN 1-931559-04-X (alk. paper)
    1. Light pollution--Environmental aspects--Juvenile literature. [1. Light pollution.] I.
Ziner, Amie, ill. II. Title.

QB51.3.L53C74 2003
522--dc22

                                                                        2003061166

                                                    ISBN: 978-1-931559-37-9 (hardcover edition)

THERE ONCE WAS A SKY FULL OF *stars*

Words by Bob Crelin
Pictures by Amie Ziner

Sky & Telescope Media, LLC
Cambridge, MA

There once was a sky full of stars,
before lighting the roadways for cars.
The worlds far away
would come out to play,
like Jupiter, Venus, and Mars.

The Milky Way stretched overhead,
once the Sun had retired to bed.
Its soft cotton glow,
like a river of snow,
looked so close it could tickle your head.

Deep, deep, out into space,
your eyes could look on to no end.
At the edge of your sight,
a galaxy's light
that took 2 million light-years to send.

The magical Moon would light up a room
and turn yards into dreamlands below.
Above where you are
a bright shooting star
bursting quick in a bright, bluish glow.

So, why are these wonders now hidden from sight?

And where did they all seem to go?

And what hides the twinkling starlight we seek

in a sky full of pink-orange glow?

Lights, lights, billions of lights
that are shining up this way and that,
lighting up flagpoles and buildings and signs
and treetops and belfries and bats!

And the universe fades on away,
if we turn all our nights into day.
Some children won't care
to look up in the air.
"Those stars are just stories," they'll say.

And what of our animal friends?
      On the night their survival depends.
Darkness tells them to sleep,
when to hunt, when to eat,
without dark . . . the one life they know ends.

The trees may not know when it's fall,
full of leaves when the winter winds call.
Although people can change
when the world's rearranged,
Mother Nature might falter and stall.

But our sky full of stars that we've hidden from sight
will once again truly be found,
when the glaring and blaring of each upward light
is turned downward to shine on the ground.

Then the Milky Way once again shines,
over star-freckled skylines, divine!
And the nights will be dark
in each forest and park,
just as in Mother Nature's design.

Yes, you and I, we can save the night sky,
the answer is simple and clear.
When we turn down the lights
that have faded our nights,
by the thousands the stars reappear.

So welcome the twilight with wide-open eyes,
under heavens unspoiled by light.
On our tiny blue world we will sail the deep skies,
as we dance with the stars in the night.

Points of Discussion

JUPITER, VENUS, AND MARS
The bright planets Jupiter, Venus, and Mars can be seen without the aid of a telescope. These nearby worlds appear like brilliant stars amongst the constellations of the zodiac.

THE MILKY WAY
The Milky Way is the enormous, star-filled galaxy that we live in. Best seen in a clear, dark sky, it appears as a glistening, cloud-like path that crosses overhead during late summer and early autumn. Its cloudy appearance is actually the light from billions and billions of stars.

SHOOTING STAR
Shooting stars are not stars at all but small, rocky debris left behind by passing comets. When these particles collide with Earth's dense atmosphere, they quickly burn up, causing a beautiful streak across the night sky. The scientific name for a shooting star is a meteor.

A GALAXY'S LIGHT
The Andromeda Galaxy is the farthest object that we can see without using a telescope or binoculars. The faint light shining from this galaxy takes nearly 2.5 million years to reach us! This extraordinary sight can be seen only if the night sky is unspoiled by light pollution.

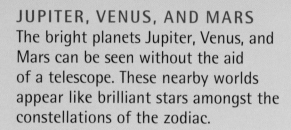

PINK-ORANGE GLOW
Sky glow is a form of light pollution that hides the stars. It's seen in the night sky above towns, cities, shopping malls, and billboards. The glow is caused by outdoor lighting that's much too bright, or by lights that shine needlessly up into the sky.

ANIMAL SURVIVAL
Animals are born with instincts that help them survive in the natural environment. Many of these instincts are in tune with the cycle of day and night. Losing night's darkness to light pollution could threaten their survival.

TREES AND LEAVES
Seasonal changes in trees and plants are determined, in part, by the natural changes in daily sunlight throughout the year. Studies have shown that artificial light shining on trees and shrubs at night can interfere with these changes.

LIGHTING FIXTURES
Many outdoor-lighting fixtures used today to light roadways, buildings, and signs also shine light up into the sky, where it serves no purpose, wastes electricity, and hides our view of the stars. Major lighting manufacturers now offer highly efficient "full cut-off" and "shielded" lighting fixtures that only shine the light downward, where it is needed. The light stays out of the sky and out of our eyes.

FIXING THE WRONGS
Many people today are unaware of how quickly we're losing the majesty of our night sky to light pollution. Most of us don't realize that by properly using outdoor light, we can fix the problem. It's up to everyone who is aware of this issue to help spread the word, save the night, and change the world.

the author

Bob Crelin has spent many years working to preserve the wonders of the night sky for our children. "There Once was a Sky Full of Stars" is his first book. He is also the author of "Faces of the Moon" (2009). An artist, inventor and musician, Bob has been providing astronomy education programs for schools, libraries and environmental groups since 1996. In 2004, Bob was honored with the Astronomical League's *Walter Scott Houston* Award. His light-pollution activism led him to design his own "night-sky friendly" light fixture for homeowners, *The GlareBuster*. On any clear night, Bob can be found sharing the stars with his family and friends.
Visit his website: www.bobcrelin.com

the illustrator

Amie Ziner is an award-winning artist and illustrator, living in CT with her husband Bill. "I'm interested in everything, especially oil painting, gardening, and cooking." She tries to make something beautiful, useful or tasty every day. See her work at amieziner.com, and watch for her new children's book, "Jennifer Ellen Watermelon."